Lea Lorena Jerns

American Literary History 1

Klausurvorbereitung in Stichpunkten

GRIN Verlag

Bibliografische Information der Deutschen Nationalbibliothek:

Die Deutsche Bibliothek verzeichnet diese Publikation in der Deutschen National-bibliografie; detaillierte bibliografische Daten sind im Internet über http://dnb.d-nb.de/ abrufbar.

Imprint:

Copyright © 2013 GRIN Verlag GmbH
Druck und Bindung: Books on Demand GmbH, Norderstedt Germany
ISBN: 978-3-656-71179-7

This book at GRIN:

http://www.grin.com/en/e-book/278071/american-literary-history-1

GRIN - Your knowledge has value

Der GRIN Verlag publiziert seit 1998 wissenschaftliche Arbeiten von Studenten, Hochschullehrern und anderen Akademikern als eBook und gedrucktes Buch. Die Verlagswebsite www.grin.com ist die ideale Plattform zur Veröffentlichung von Hausarbeiten, Abschlussarbeiten, wissenschaftlichen Aufsätzen, Dissertationen und Fachbüchern.

Visit us on the internet:

http://www.grin.com/

http://www.facebook.com/grincom

http://www.twitter.com/grin_com

American Literary History I

- 1607 Jamestown established
- when British came to North America to find gold & to discover the 2nd paradise, many different Native American people were already living there
- not only English people there, also Dutch Swedes, Spanish
- 1620: Pilgrims arrive in New England on Mayflower → COLONIAL PERIOD
- Puritans arrived some years later to spread religious and worldly ideas
→ left a great literary legacy (had a fine education system) → produced sermons, diaries

Colonial period 1607-1760s
- by 1700 laws that made slavery racial (whites not allowed to be enslaved)
- European settlements moved further to west
- in North America basically British, Spanish people

Colonial Literature
- integrated into English literary system
- content begins to reflect the move towards independence
- forms: old established literary forms like sonnets, wrote about landscape

John Smith "The General History of Virginia" (1624)
- encounter with an unfamiliar landscape, unfamiliar people
- Natives were not a united group, English were relatively few in number
- autobiography (talks about himself in 3rd person)
- geographical reference (Jamestown)
- establishing myth of Pocahontas (daughter of powerful Nat. Am king)
- was imprisoned by Powhatan (Native American king)
- thought he will be killed → but often said to have been an adoption ceremony rather than an attempt to kill him
- writes about Pocahontas saving his life and falling in love with her (but not liable)
- Pocahontas definitely married a settler → tour to England to convince more people to move to America → was a sensation in England, was received by king → died before travelling back to America
- dramatization → may have felt intimidated
- demonization → fear of foreigners
- Natives are presented like stereotypes
- 3rd person narrative but nevertheless personal opinions, judgements
- Pocahontas sacrifices herself for white man → whites are superior → glorification of colonial policy, success of colonial policy
- text as means of propaganda: marriage with native woman to get territory of Natives
- happy ending, but weak woman dies → symbol for downfall of Natives

Mary Rowlandson "A Narrative of the Captivity and Restoration" (1682)
- captivity narrative (having been kept by natives and then released → writing about experiences)
- was caught by Nat. Am. For 12 weeks (part of her family was killed)
- wrote a very detailed account of her time in captivity (structured in geographically)
- she returned to Puritan community (but many others who were caught decided not to return

1

and stayed with Natives)
- negative description of the Natives (barbarian)

→Natives are brutal, shoot with weapons of British people → but description from only one perspective → doesn't describe how British people fight back
- her victim role (which was created by herself) justifies how Natives were treated
- calls Natives master&mistress → justification for slavery
- positive picture of Puritans
- tells that God saved her, compares herself with biblical figures
- sticks to her religion although she could have stayed there → people at home should be proud of her
- strength of woman → emphasizes pride of whites
- motive: revenge → political propaganda
- story was addressed primarily to Puritans (God saved her, proof of her faith) but also 2nd audience in England
- religious form allowed her to publish the narrative even though she is woman

Revolutionary Period (1760s-80s)
- 1776 Declaration of Independence
- 1789 Constitution
- authors often politicians, wrote autobiographies

18th century American Literature
- influence of enlightenment and natural rights philosophy → people have certain rights because they were born
- belief in power of reason, perfectibility of mankind
- high literacy rates to be able to read Bible
- Benjamin Franklin: paper money, argued that colonies needed own money, essays how to become wealthy, became rich through writing, set down principles he followed every day, structured his day precisely
- Thomas Paine: propagated advantages of Independence
- Thomas Jefferson: one writer of Declaration of Independence, supported enlightenment, sets up constitution of US, state and church should be separate, liberation of slaves

Literature of the Early Republic (1790s-1820s) / Early American Drama
- overall theme: question of national identity, defining an American national identity
- entertainment (different from European theatre)
- rich people sat in special places/balconies → social segregation
- pamphlets how to behave in theatre itself
- author totally insignificant, actors were important
- no ideas of originality
- parts of Shakespeare plays were performed
- melodrama (play with music)

→ dominant dramatic form of 19th century, stock characters, developed in Europe, moral contrast between good and bad, happy ending, technical sophistication (real fire, real water falls)
- 19th century: Indian plays popular e.g. James Nelson Barker

- time around Am.Rev. Natives lost a lot of land → sold to European settlers
- Natives pushed westwards
- European Am. Sometimes presented themselves as Native Am. To distinguish themselves from English, claim certain identity

Transcendentalism 1830s-150s
- link to American drama: search for American identity
- term based on Kant
- relation to British Romanticism
- strongly opposed to increasing materialism of their time
- against rationalism
- rationality is limited → more spiritual understanding of the world
- importance of individualism
- critique on contemporary society
- attraction of alternative life-styles
- texts: speeches, essays, sermons, diaries, lectures → non-fictional texts
- characteristic: openness of texts, hybrid texts, between theology, philosophy and poetry, pragmatism
- oversoul → self → nature → oversoul...
- nature: central sphere of influence where knowledge-formation takes place → new form of religiosity
- e.g. Ralph Waldo Emerson, Henry David Thoreau, Margaret Fuller

Henry David Thoreau "Resistance to Civil Government"
- essay
- experience of spending a night in jail → refused to pay taxes
- everybody should follow his/her conscience, even though it is in conflict with law
- dreams of Middle Ages in prison (time that America never had) → Europoean ideals
- heroic character
- anti-materialistic view
- everyone has the right to express his opinion and participate in a revolution
- compares government with with a machine that should be stopped when it doesn't work properly anymore
- everyone should stand up for justice
- many people are against slavery and Mexican war, but do not get active
- majority should not decide upon everything (voting in not enough)
- prison: right place bc. One is locked out of the state
- democracy is not the best form of government
- "I quietly declare war with the state!"

Early American Short Story
- no American invention
- Edgar Allan Poe tried to define the genre
- publication in journals: writing became job (Washington Irving)

Edgar Allan Poe
- theory about short stories
- poetry and short story: aesthetic, emotional, not about truth/facts
- repetitions/variation of application
- to achieve unity of a text, it should be possible to read it in one session
- should be characterized by economy (every word, sentence has a function)
- climatic conclusion at the end
- totality or unity of effect → all parts of text contribute to unity
- air of consequence or causation
- composition comparable to a mathematical problem

- beauty, the elevation of the soul is the province of poetry
- melancholy is the most legitimate poetical tone
- most pertinent object of contemplation: death of a beautiful woman

→ *"The Fall of the House of Usher" (1839)*
- gothic tale, connected to Middle Ages
- evoking terror → own smallness with regard to the universe
- psychology is used to create effects of fear
- 1st person narrator who experiences strange things in a house
- atmosphere evoked by adjectives
- vivid description of landscape
- house mirrors the psychological state of the characters
- tale within a tale → narrator tells brother a tale of Middle Ages
- symbols/metaphors
- brother+sister last descendants of house of Usher → sisters dies → brother carries her to the grave in a very stormy night → but sister revives → both die
- narrator flees → house breaks down behind him → symbol for downfall of last descendants
- connection to incest? → descendants die before impurification possible
- house of usher=breakdown of England, of nobility, but America can escape (there is no nobility), even in England ideological incest
- stream in front of house=Atlantic Ocean between England and America
- narrator plays crucial role: boundary reality-story → narrator tries to find rational explanation for spooky phenomena, but fails

→ *"The Tell-Tale Heart" (1835)*
- 1st person narrator → insanity, madness
- eyes as a symbol for hell
- eyes of a vulture → wheels around death
- blind eye can't see him, because it is blind, but has the thought of being watched
- wants to blind eye with lamp at midnight, but eye does not react
- individualism vs. controlling eye
- old father is watching you!

American Renaissance 1850s-70s

The early US-American novel
sentimental novel
- English traditions
- response to the enlightenment's emphasis on rationality
- affirmation of social feelings as sources of moral behaviour
- pity for and empathy with the weak: women, children, slaves, Natives
- frequently written by women
- ideology of separate spheres/cult of true womanhood → male and female spheres are divided, geographical separation (women at home, men at work), men and women culturally distinct, people who did not conform to the model were not fully human (e.g. Natives)
- highly political (abolitionist movement increased, slavery presented as a national problem)
- tears can create solidarity → outward sign for an inner change
- e.g. Harriet Beecher Stowe
picaresque novel
gothic novel

4

historical novel
- written from perspective of 19th century, attempt to reinterpret American past

Harriet Beecher Stowe "Uncle Tom's Cabin" (1852)
- very popular in 19th century
- sentimental novel, no slave narrative
- family of slaveholders indebted → have to sell slaves
- slave Eliza flees, because master wants to sell her son → jumps in a river between 2 states (in one state slavery is prohibited) → senator helps her (passed bloodhound law--> it is not allowed to help slaves to escape)
- Uncle Tom: do not condemn your master, pray for them → believes in the good of men
- Uncle Tom is one of the slaves → sold → mistreated, dies
- institution of slavery destroys family bonds
- Uncle Tom = Christlike figure → sacrificed himself for others, represents Christian morality, Af. American can be culturally equal to whites
- audience: white readers/white women
- main topic: Loss of a child → experiences made whites feel with black parents because child mortality high in those days, identification with protagonists
- significance of tears
- mobilizing the ideology of separate spheres for the abolition of slavery
- not very liable, many actions in short time, but nevertheless pathetic

Early Feminist Novel
- middle of 19th century: 1st American feminist movement (also active in abolitionist movement)
- 1848: Seneca Falls Convention (argued for equal rights for women)

Slave Narratives
development of slavery
- established in all British colonies before independence
- after independence: in Northern part slavery vanished, in the South even stronger
- Northern parts: abolitionist movement
- great impact on American literary history

slave narratives
- form of autobiography
- 1st person accounts of life under slavery, generally by fugitive slaves
- importance of factuality and reliability → prefaces and afterwords
- influence on later African American literature
- genesis of Realism
- central theme: literacy and freedom
- emancipation: slaves could write down their experience
- important gender differences
- political aim: ????

Harriet Jacobs "Incidents in the Life of a Slave girl" (1861)
- protagonist is slave since her birth, but didn't know it until she was 6 years old
- was sexually abused by her master
- escaped the treatment by having an affair with a white man (but she loved a black man)
- had 2 children with white man → he bought his children, remained slaves

- escaped to her grandmother's house, later escaped to North → white woman bought her freedom
- dreamed of an own house, but no money, not married → didn't achieve privileges that would go along with femininity
- worked as a servant for the woman who bought her freedom → to be free doesn't mean to achieve complete independence → one is born as a slave and dies as a slave
- topics: freedom, , emphasize of religion (quotes from bible)
- religion, bible used for legitimation of slavery → people serve other people
- religion=white system → Jacobs applies to white system to get freedom → is allowed to christen her children → triumph over whites
- motive: compassion → wants to be pitied, recognized as a human being

<u>Early African American Novelists</u>
- e.g. William Wells Brown, Harriet E. Wilson
- The Fireside Poets: against slavery, theme=Natives

Walt Whitman "Song of Myself" (1855) (Transcendentalism)
- wrote a number of quite conventional texts
- part of "Leaves of a Grass"
- topics: God as abstract concept that is in everyone, search for the own limits, democracy, patriotism, slavery
- writes about himself
- free verse=new kind of form, no rhyme, flexible, has rhythm
- personalizes lyrical I, is always in dialogue with a "you" → reader feels involved
- comprehensive poem about America
- grass=central symbol → importance of nature, a collective thing consisting of individual parts, green=colour of hope, optimism, grows everywhere → democratic, all people have relation to it
- positive, optimistic tone → great hopes for USA as a nation and the role for the individual in that nation
- lyrical I as part of a collective
- offers many different interpretations

<u>Female Poets</u>
- mid 19th century
- domestic topics, sentimental influence

Emily Dickinson poems
- adapted structure of church hymns (clearly defined stanzas, rhyme)
- innovative punctuation and capitalization, spell things in unusual way
- elliptical
- amazing opposites open up different ways of interpretation
- poems have numbers, no titles
- hyphens → connects and separates, silence,
→ 510 "It was not death"
- motive: depression, hopelessness, desperation
- confused thoughts, but very strict order of poem
- emotional
- narrator lives at cemetery → death is everyday topic
- lives social death

→ 712
- death picks up persona with carriage → death, funeral
- eternity and mortality are no contrast
- not depressive, rather calm, forgiving
- erotic tension between male death and female persona
- slaves watch her passing by → are very close to death as well
- death is her life, comes like a prince with a carriage, desire

→ "I heard a fly buzz"
- persona on death bed
- death as the beginning of eternal life in afterlife
- fly = connection between life and death, companion on her way to afterlife
- fly=normal → normalization of death
- persona waits for king on death bed, but fly arrives → irony
- death present bc. Of civil war → very frequent motive
- death as liberation from earthly suffering

Herman Melville "Bartleby, the Scrivener" (1853)
- Wall street: financial centre
- Bartleby: not focused on work "I prefer not to", refuses work, shows no emotions
- lawyer finds out that Barleby lives in office → compassion
- Bartleby is fired, but refuses to leave → lawyer moves to another office
- new lawyer gives Bartleby in charge → dies in prison because he refused to eat
- Bartleby worked in dead letters office → his work has dead end → he is surrogate for dead people, receives their letters → is himself dead
- Bartleby is anti-wallstreet → against economic growth, refuses work, but is imprisoned there bc. Of large walls
- "I would prefer not to" very polite, doesn't refuse directly
- Bartleby is like a machine, but human because he is the only one who opposes the striving for money, luck
- critique an capitalism, industrialization → weak people have no chance in capitalistic world

1861-65 Civil War
afterwards:
- slavery fully abolished
- African Americans were granted more rights (but only for a short period of time) → perios of reconstruction: African Americans held important political positions
- racism didn't come to an end, got even worse
- 3 commendments to constitution
- new techological inventions
- US became an increasingly urban country
- increasing social division (rich-poor)
- women began to enter male sphere (got active in social work)

Realism 1870s-1918
- understanding of reality based on experience and observation (empirical, positivist)
- against idealization and falsification of experiences
- against the romance, melodrama, sentimental novel
- happy endings rare

- more restraint tone
- from omniscient narrator to 3rd person narrator (impression of objectivity and immediacy)
- wealth of detail
- from heroic to everyday characters → predominantly white middle class
- complex characters instead of stereotypes → make mistakes, learn, are ambivalent
- simple, descriptive instead of poetic language
- openness of literary form
- more active role of the reader → balance of pain and pleasure in the texts, close to reader's own life
- people from different social backgrounds coming together (old money vs. new money, Europe vs. America)→ have to learn how to understand each other, no prejudices
- centrality of marriage plot
- deconstruction of false images with regard to race and slavery
- demonstration of injustice of racial prejudice
- cultural capital counts, not only money → texts should produce cultural capital in the reader
→ education through reading

historical context:
- after Civil War army started fighting against Native Americans → Natives pushed back to reservation
- whites eradicated N.A. Culture
- extended their territory by means of violence
- 1900 lowest point of N.A. Population in the US

Henry James "The Real Thing" (1892)
- narrator is painter → couple of monarchs offers themselves for his romantic paintings → are the real thing because she is a real lady and he is a real gentleman → but they a very static, not flexible
- Painter fires couple and taxes new couple (opposite to old couple) → monarchs have no value in a world, which sticks to the exterior
- monarchs are the real thing because they are unchangeable
- behave like puppets → artificial, not real, no empathy→ irony
- were very rich, but now social decline → their appearance is kept
- story very socio-critical

<u>Local Color Writing /Literary Regionalism</u>
- part of realism
- focus on specific regions of the US with different subject matters
- detailed rendition of regions and people (language of particular regions) → careful representation of dialect (based on oral narration)
- 1st person narrator
- revitalizing literary language
- specific forms in the South, New England and the West
- critical view on the regions
- many of the authors were women
- dealing with scarcity of resources → scarcity of language
- e.g. Mark Twain "Huckleberry Finn"
- mostly perspective of white authors
- different views by non-white authors

Native American Literature
- oral tradition, often personal experiences
- more N.A. Began to write when whites tried to suppress their culture
- importance of autobiography → written to a white writer

S. Alice Callaham "Wynema" (1891)
- of mixed race, tried to suggest to white readership that N.A. Can be civilized
- Turn to current political events of the time: 1887 Dawes Act, Allotment Act → attempt to destroy part of N.A. Culture, each Native family got a small piece of land (expected to have farms and get americanized), land not taken away violently
- Wynema: wants Western education in her reservation → learns English, wants to become teacher
- white teacher Genevieve (missionary) lives with Wynema → takes her to her white family
- Wynema falls in love with her brother → marriage, Allotment Act, many people killed in fights
- fictionalized version of the "Massacre of Wounded Knee's" → white soldiers killed about 300 N.A.
- Genevieve refuses marriage with white because he is racist
- Wynema embodies Native traditions, but also assimilation to white culture
- Sentimental novel: compassion, focus on weak persons (women)
- topics: tolerance, equality, love
- still Genevieve feels superior, hierachical, Natives presented as uncivilized

Literature by Immigrants
- immigrants were looked at with suspicion by Americans (weren't sure whether they should be considered as whites)
- Jewish writers: Emma Lazarus, Abraham Cahan
- multiculturalism in literature → impact of migration and ethnic diversity
- Chinese-American Literature

Naturalism 1890s-1900
historical context
- emerged around 1900
- embedded in political and social context: reference to Guilded Age (disparities rich-poor)
- beginnings of social work
- attempts to limit power of great companies
- better working conditions, no child labour
- age of Imperialism
- professionalization of publishing sector
- new kinds of newspapers (directed to large readership)
- gender: women began to move into public sphere (higher education)
- sports became accessible to larger party of the population
- new ideas of masculinity: men's body should reflect character (body building)

literature
- as a continuation of Realism
- against idealization
- wealth of factual detail (dialect etc.)
- expansion of literary subject matter: lower class characters, slums
- social groups that were excluded from literature before, lower classes are focused

- different understanding of reality than in Realism
- plot of exhaustion, degeneration (frequently characters die, plot of decline
- biological model of reality → Social Darwinism (individuals who prosper are well adapted)
- everybody dependent on himself, no state support
- everybody determined by their environment
- focus on matter beyond the reach of civilization: heritage, sex, money, primitive desire, the milieu
- mainly male authors, white
- male characters in a crisis → narrator superior, has complete control
- relation narrator&character: narrator has great distance, controls characters (comments of behaviour), but narrator as well identifies with characters
- influence of European Naturalism (the author as scientist)
- bifurcated role of the narrator: between a limited and incomprehensive stance and critical distance
- narrative irony
- metaphorical language

Transformations of cities
- infrastructure revolution
- cities extended geographically (people were mobile due to new means of transport)
- electric trams/cable cars
- sky scraper, new building techniques
- cultural movement: cities should look nice, be aesthetic for people
- 1890s women entered labour market on large scale

Theodore Dreiser "Sister Carrie" (1900)
- one of the classic Naturalist novels
- classic x-shaped plot
- Sister Carrie rises, male character declines (suicide)
- fallen woman from countryside comes to the city → doesn't get married, rises through institution of theatre → fascinates the audience with her theatre performance
- woman manages to become rich → makes career in the sphere of representation rather in the productive sphere

Pre-Modernism/Early Modernism 1900-1918
- urbanization, industrialization, multiculturalism, transformation of capitalism, growth of consumer society
- new woman: working, is mobile
- increasing respectability of divorce

Charlotte Perkins Gilman "The Yellow Wallpaper" (1892)
- part of suffrage movement, edited her own journal
- short story, 1st person journal entries
- protagonists husband thinks her to be depressive, mentally ill → has to go to hospital, chained to her bed
- describes yellow wallpaper → wallpaper changes, smells strange
- dreams that wallpaper is alive, becomes a woman → wants to release woman, breaks down the wallpaper
- gender: just male persons around her
- wallpaper reflects her illness → loses contact to outside world, lives in own world

- lives in captivity → like woman in wallpaper → become one person
- pattern on wallpaper turn out to be bars at night
- environment: old country estate, gothic surrounding, colonial style → Indians keep on and on, ghosts of Natives are there → want revenge → protagonists doesn't find silence
- Natives were imprisoned, woman also gets imprisoned → suffering ignored
- her baby is male → rejects him → feminism → permanently controlled by men
- wallpaper as projection surface → film
- link to jaundice (Gelbsucht) → spreads through immigrants
- yellow → Asian people migrated to America → not welcome → breaks down wallpaper → Asian people should go

W.E.B. Du Bois "The Souls of Black Folk" (1903)
- challenged segregation in court, challenged discrimination laws
- difficult to classify
- partly autobiographical
- spiritual sorrow songs → great grief expressed
- language very polite, not aggressive but pleading
- double-consciousness: position as African American and at the same time American, twoness
→ difference: perception of how they see themselves and how they are seen by others
- chapter headings: musical score, poetry by Euopean writers → implicit argument that Af.Am. Culture is as valuable as the most highly esteemed Western pieces of art
- beginning: 1st person narration, then "you", then "we" → unity, first rather autobiography
- spirituals: to awake associations, support for community